MY HEART
Rejoices

Created and Produced by Russell Mauldin

14 SAB ARRANGEMENTS

ARRANGED BY CAMP KIRKLAND · TOM FETTKE · LARI GOSS · BRUCE GREER ·

CINDY BERRY · KEITH CHRISTOPHER · DAVE WILLIAMSON · CLAUDE BASS ·

BILL WOLAVER · RANDY SMITH · MARTY HAMBY · TIM AYERS · DOUG HOLCK

Vocals adapted by Randy Smith

Companion Products Available:

Listening Cassette 0-7673-3169-9

Accompaniment Cassette 0-7673-3170-2
(Contains both Split-track and Stereo Tracks)

Accompaniment CD 0-7673-3171-0 (Split-track)

Individual Orchestrations Available

GENEVOX

0-7673-3168-0

Foreword

One of the more challenging responsibilities of any church music leader is trying to find appropriate music for the choir. I always ask myself several questions about the music I consider. (1) What type of service will it be appropriate for: thematic, seasonal, or general, and does the text have a theologically sound message that the church and choir need to hear? (2) What are the voice parts like: can my choir members execute the ranges required? (3) How much rehearsal time will it take to rehearse each selection? (4) Can my accompanists play the music, and, if not, are tasteful accompaniment tracks in CD and cassette format available? And, last but not least, (5) Will my choir enjoy singing these songs?

As you examine *My Heart Rejoices*, I think you'll be able to respond positively to each of the questions above. This delightful collection represents 14 of the best contemporary Christian songs around, written by composers you'll both recognize and appreciate. The melodies are memorable, rescored for SAB voicing, yet retaining the full integrity of the original harmonic structures. The messages are meaningful, each clear and concise. And the many ways you'll find to use the music is measureless. From the swelling praise of Cindy Berry's "I Worship You," to the quiet statement of adoration of Bruce Greer's "My Savior's Love" to Randy Smith's setting of the high-energy spiritual, "Victory Shall Be Mine," you'll find music in this collection suitable for a wide variety of uses.

My Heart Rejoices will be a collection you'll turn to again and again as you seek to lead your choir and congregation in special times of praise and worship. May your hearts truly rejoice as you sing of His wonderful love.

Danny R. Jones, Consultant
Smaller Church Music Ministries
Music Ministries Department
Sunday School Board of
the Southern Baptist Convention

Contents

*Commissioned for the
Southern Baptist Church Music Conference,
Atlanta, 1995*

I Worship You
(With Songs of Praise)

Words and Music by
CINDY BERRY
Vocals adapted by Randy Smith

Here am I, ho-ly Lord, seek-ing now Your face,

thank-ful for Your grace, as I wor-ship You.

Here am I, ho-ly Lord, in this qui-et hour.

By Your Spir-it's pow'r, cleanse my heart a-new. O

Lamb of God, the One that I a-dore, a-dore, I

6

long to sing Your praise for - ev - er - more. _____ I

wor - ship You _____ with songs of praise; _____ in

You a - lone _____ my heart re - joic - es. _____ Ac -

8

Lead me in Your ways, as I seek to praise and mag - ni -

With more strength

fy Your name. Might-y King, Lord of all, I

stand in awe of You. Faith - ful, just, and true, You're ev - er -

9

Victory Shall Be Mine

Words and Music by
NANCY HARMON
Arr. by Randy Smith

15

18

Each One, Reach One
with
Share Jesus Now

Words and Music by
BABBIE MASON
Arranged by Camp Kirkland
Vocals adapted by Randy Smith

*Share Je - sus now, Share Je - sus now,

In ev - 'ry place, in ev - 'ry way that you know how.

*"Share Jesus Now" is ideal for congregational use with accompaniment concluding on the downbeat chord of Ms. 19.

27

My Savior's Love

with

I Stand Amazed in the Presence

KEITH FERGUSON

BRUCE GREER

34

with growing intensity

My Sav - ior's love— does not de - pend on my faith - less heart; It de - pends on Him!

*How mar - vel-ous! how won - der-ful! And my song shall

* "I Stand Amazed in the Presence" Words and Music by CHARLES H. GABRIEL.

38

Jesus, Thou Joy of Loving Hearts

BERNARD of CLAIRVAUX
Translated by Ray Palmer

CLAUDE L. BASS
Vocals adapted by Randy Smith

42

change - ful lot is ___ cast; ___

Glad when Thy gra - cious smile we see, ___

Blest when our faith can hold Thee fast.

That All May Know

JEFF SWITZER and JIM PARIS

JEFF SWITZER
Arranged by Keith Christopher
Vocals adapted by Randy Smith

15 know" _____ be - came His sto - ry.   unis.

"That all may know" be - came His sto - ry.   Sins washed a -

G/B   Dm7/A   G   F/C   C   Am7   G/B

cresc.

17   mf   CD:21 2nd time   Second time to Coda ⊕

way _____ whit - er than snow;   The price He

mf   Second time to Coda ⊕

C2   C   C/E   Dm7/F   A7/E   Dm7   Em7   F

mf

19   mp

paid _____ that all may know.

mp

C/G   C2/G   C   N.C.

mp

50

Bless the Lord

I Will Bless Thee, O Lord
I Will Bless You, Lord
I Will Bless the Lord

Arranged by Dave Williamson
Vocals adapted by Randy Smith

WORSHIP LEADER (optional): (1st time) Welcome, Church! We've come together today for a wonderful purpose—to celebrate the life of our living Lord! To thank Him for all He's done and to praise Him for all that He is, let's bless His name together!

(2nd time) O Church—God's Word tells us that if we fail to praise Him, the very rocks will fill the void and cry out, "Hosanna!" It's time to join as one voice and sing!

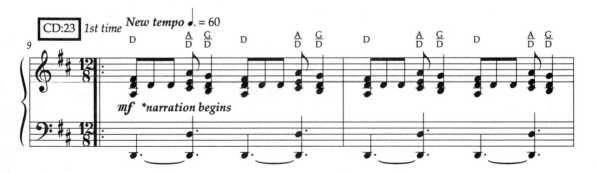

56

60

*"I Will Bless the Lord"

Slower tempo

I will bless the Lord and give Him glo - ry; Oh,— I

Jesus Saves

Words and Music by
ROGER AND DEBBIE BENNETT
Choral Arr. by Bill Wolaver
Orchestrated by Lari Goss
Vocals adapted by Randy Smith

68

CD:30

73

74

* "We Have Heard the Joyful Sound" Words by PRISCILLA OWENS. Music by WILLIAM J. KIRKPATRICK.

world will hear_ my voice, Je - sus saves!_____ The

world will hear_ my voice, Je - sus saves!

Je - sus_ saves!_____

Jesus Is Lord of All
with
He Is Lord

Words and Music by
LEROY McCLARD
Arranged by Camp Kirkland
Vocals adapted by Randy Smith

*"He Is Lord," Traditional. Arrangement © Van Ness Press, Inc. (ASCAP).

82

84

To Rescue a Sinner Like Me

Words and Music by
GLENN CALCOTE
Arranged by Camp Kirkland
Vocals adapted by Randy Smith

90

130

He a - ban-doned His throne and His king-dom a - bove To

A7sus A7   G   D2/F♯   G2   D2/F♯

135

res - cue a sin - ner like me. He a - ban-doned His

Em7   Em7/A   A♯°7 Bm   Bm/A   G2

dim.   *mf*

140

throne   To res - cue   a

and His king-dom a - bove

D2/F♯   G2   D2/F♯   Em7   Em7

dim.

dim.

Remember Me

JAMES L. DARBY
Arranged by Camp Kirkland and Tom Fettke
Vocals adapted by Randy Smith

What a Wonderful Lord

Words and Music by
TIM AYERS
Vocals adapted by Randy Smith

In my heart there is pur - pose to
pure._____ Oo_____

praise You ev - 'ry day,— So I can face an - y fear— with faith— se -
Oo_____ Ah_____

CD:44

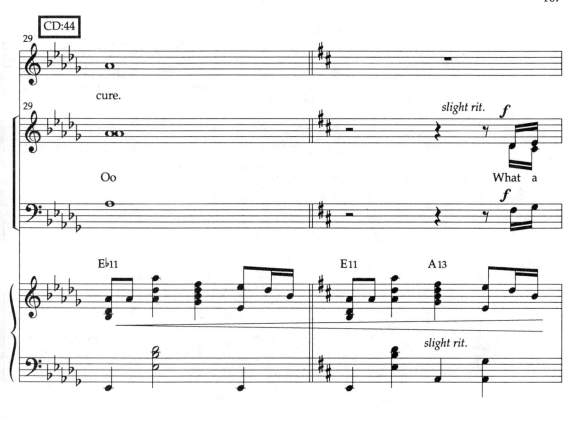

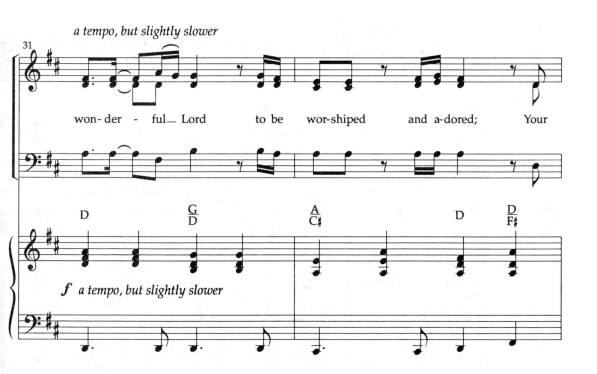

Cast All Your Cares

Words and Music by
CAROL CYMBALA
Arranged by Doug Holck
Vocals adapted by Randy Smith

116

118

Without Him

Words and Music by
MYLON R. LeFEVRE
Arranged by Marty Hamby
Vocals adapted by Randy Smith

First time - CHOIR
Second time - SOLO

1. With - out Him I could do noth - ing. ____
(2. With) - out Him I would be dy - ing. ____

____ With - out Him ____ I'd sure - ly fail; ____
____ With - out Him ____ I'd be en - slaved; ____

*Useful when anthem is used as an invitational number. Verses and choruses may be repeated as needed.

128